Thoughts are Everything

Valerie Hare

Sushana Press

ISBN 978-1-9196408-0-8

Cover artwork by Valerie Hare

It's all about you.

You having more fun, more love, more health, more wealth.

Putting these thoughts & ideas into practice has helped us & the people we work with achieve a degree of success in life & happiness that previously seemed elusive. Have a go: hopefully they'll do the same for you too.

We'll be looking at questions like:

Do you love what you do ?

Do you love where you live ?

Do you love who you live with ?

. . . If not then why not ??

Most of us spend our lives pleasing other people mostly out of fear: fear of losing their love, their approval, or perhaps our own security.

Hopefully this book will help you feel more secure in every area of your life, because your security will be in the universe & yourself rather than in other people.

Because you'll be thinking about you, this doesn't mean you'll be abandoning everyone. It just means you'll be putting yourself first (shock horror) & considering yourself at least as much as you consider others.

We are taught that this is a selfish way to be . . . . . . but once you start doing this, you will be happier, which means you will be healthier, have more energy & be more fun to be around . . . . . If you take care of yourself first, you won't need anyone to look after you.

If you are doing a job you love & would do it anyway whether you were paid or not, you will be financially secure . . . you won't need anyone to provide for you.

If you love yourself & know what makes you happy, you will be a magnetic, fun person & attract all sorts of wonderful like-minded people. You will have a happy, fulfilled life all the time whether you are alone or with others . . . you get to choose.

To do this doesn't mean you have to abandon the life you have in front of you. Nothing has gone wrong, it's just that what you were thinking about . . . . . paying attention to . . . . . you have created & it's now in front of you !

If you were thinking about debt & struggle, more came.
If you were thinking about pressure, more came.
If you were thinking about loneliness, more came.

What you are thinking about you'll get more of, so . . . . . If you start thinking about what you want, you can recreate your life at any moment . . . . . Which moment are you going to choose?

As soon as you start to change your thoughts, focusing upon what you want, your life will immediately start to reflect this back to you & then you are on your way.

A good way to make a start is to find something in your life you love, anything.

A hug from your friend, your wife, your husband, your baby's smile . . . . . seeing your dog leap up & down with joy to see you . . . . . anything . . . . . just find something to appreciate & slowly you'll recreate your life to what you want.

Rather than events just randomly appearing, you will start to realise that you are in control of the way it is all unfolding & you will start to see that your thoughts about your life are what determines the content of it . . . . . Now you're starting to cook with gas & can create anything you want . . . . . knowing that what you give your attention to you'll get more of.

Over the weeks we'll remind you that you know all this stuff, deep down, you've just forgotten. The ideas will start to fit into place like jigsaw puzzle pieces. You'll begin to see where you need to make changes in your thinking to create the life you want.

Although the same principles, the fact that what you think about you'll get more of –

(so . . . . . make sure the majority of your thoughts are good ones)

apply to any area of your life,

we will cover all areas: relationships, health, financial security, fulfilling your life purpose & more . . . . .

So good luck & have fun !

Daily affirmations
and
Weekly Wonders

Daily affirmations, week 1

Theme: Happiness.

1

Next step always gives a skip to your heart.

2

First I'm going to be very, very happy. Then do everything I have to do after that.

3

Whenever you have a dream, a wish or a desire, you always have the wherewithal to achieve it.

4

Say "I now HAVE" rather than "I want" otherwise you'll always remain wanting.
Feel how good it is to have it, pretend it's here. It has to come !

5

In any situation ask what can I give here, not what can I get. It will come back 100 times... not necessarily from where you gave it.

Your Weekly Wonder 1

In relationships we are all sure we are right and the other person is wrong, but we are all right: everyone has a point of view that needs to be heard.

Everyone, all of us, just wants to be loved and accepted exactly the way we are without having to fit in and turn ourselves into a pretzel to be appreciated and noticed.

We are perfect just the way we are. We don't need to apologise for behaving in a way that makes us feel the happiest.

To be able to live like this we must see that everyone else also wants this.

We need to accept that everyone round us is entitled also to have everything the way they want without having to turn themselves into a pretzel for us.

They also have a point of view and their point of view is just as valid as ours, just different, even if we don't accept or 'get' it.

This is what we need to understand and accept to have harmony.

This year we need to stop having to be right and choose to be happy.

Only you can do this, and yes you can do it now, without any person or circumstance having to change.

If you don't make a decision to be happy you never will be.

You will always need people or circumstances to be a certain way, otherwise you will be disappointed; and as there is no guarantee that they will behave in that way, or even if they do, that it will be for very long, you are likely to be disappointed unless you choose to make a decision to be happy, no matter what, no matter what.

Happiness is an inside job.

Once you choose to be happy, the universe will send you things to be happy about.

Most of us are doing it the opposite way. We are waiting for someone to change or something to step in that makes us happy. We may be waiting a long time for this.

The secret is, decide to feel happy first, no matter what is in front of you, and then watch the magic step in to bring to you what is guaranteed to bring you happiness.

The first step has to come from you. The universe will then take sixteen to help. It may not be the way you expect, but it is a guarantee that whatever then steps in will bring you far greater joy than you could possibly have imagined.

Daily affirmations, week 2

1

If you're happy, everyone around you will be happy. Your joy and happiness will help others, your complaining won't.

2

Miracles are everyday occurrences. Live as though you really believe that whatever it is you are asking for is on its way. Prepare for it in whatever way you can. IT HAS TO COME.

3

You will be successful the moment you let go of the thoughts of NOT being successful. Stay focused on what it is you WANT . . . You get what you concentrate on, stay with the good.

4

*How much do you want? All of it? OK. There is
no limit, but you have to believe it is possible for
you and live as though you already have it in
whatever way you can. Start small, think big.*

5

Take a minute just to be.

Your Weekly Wonder 2

Most of us learn throughout life about what we will and won't put up with regarding relationships of all kinds.

Make a decision to step into a new age which highlights you, where you show more respect for yourself, therefore drawing more respect from others to you.

Be more aware that, above all, we want peace and harmony in our relationships and lives on every level. Genuine peace and harmony. Be no longer willing to make huge allowances for people, condoning bad behaviour, continually turning things round, this all ends.

Try very hard during the next few weeks to accelerate this way of living into your world, as a permanent state, by pausing and thinking now, before reacting to difficult people. Loving them for their lack of insight and ability to behave in a loving way will disarm them and initiate a change in the way they react to you. You will dissipate and dissolve any damaging interactions between you and others and all caustic energy and disruption will begin to dissolve.

As you keep your thoughts towards peace, tranquility and good relations and accept nothing less, this will become your natural state of being. . . . . HALLELUJAH !

Daily affirmations, week 3

1

You have within you all the knowledge & tools you need to make a success of your life this time round.

2

You will never be sent more than you can cope with. If you feel overwhelmed by work, stop & decide what really has to be done today, you'll find there's always time for what has to be done.

3

If you come up against closed doors in life, don't bang on them. Go to the ones that open easily.

4

If something doesn't work out the way you planned, it's because there's something far better for you. You were just not asking for enough.

5

Don't limit yourself to a certain job, house or person; let the universe sort the details. There could be something far more amazing planned for you.

Your Weekly Wonder 3

Chaos is often rife, but this is always a good thing. When we are confused we have no idea of how things are going to work out, and therefore we lose any attachment to the end result because we just don't know.

This is a magical time because once our human hands let go of how things 'ought' to be, the universe can intervene, knowing all the desires we have thrown out earlier, and can start its magic, drawing to us what we most want.

You will notice a lot more synchronicity than ever before, confirmation that we are on track with our desires and the universe is joining up all the dots to bring our dreams to us.

When it seems turbulent and there is a lot of confusion around, look for a sense of hope and optimism and a quiet knowing, a great sense of anticipation about the future. On some level we can all feel our good is here now, waiting to step in.

Living as you will when it arrives is the fast forward button to draw it to you.

This is the secret, start living as though you have a written guarantee that what you have asked for has been granted.

You are then on the same vibration to magnetize it to you.

So press it NOW.

Daily affirmations, week 4

1

Try & do what you want to do rather than what you feel you ought to do whenever you can.

2

In situations where it seems impossible to do what you would like to do, change your attitude towards it.

3

See the good in everything, everywhere, there is so much good. Concentrate on it , the rest will fall away.

4

In the moment you see what you don't want, you'll immediately see what you do want (the opposite).

5

When you do what you want to do rather than what you feel you ought to do, you will find that it always works better for everyone.

Your Weekly Wonder 4

Try only to spend time with people who want to be with you. If you have to continually call people and hope they will call back, let them go.

There is a subtle difference here, with you perhaps pursuing someone who is just a lot busier than you are at the moment, but you always 'know' what the truth of a situation is.

Start to honour yourself and spend time only with people who seek you out and want to be with you.

Knock only on doors that are opening.

Start to appreciate what you have in front of you, that which you have already created. This will cause more to come to you that will make you happy and appreciative. You don't even need to know what you want. The universe has heard your every desire and will send what is appropriate. Your job is only to spend no time noticing what is 'missing' and all the time finding something, anything, to enjoy.

Hidden in every desire you have, there is always the way to achieve it.

You have heard the sayings 'money comes to money', 'like attracts like', 'what goes around comes around'. These old wives' tales are full of truth and promise on how to live life.

Be joyful, be appreciative, so like a magnet you will draw in more to be joyful about. Kick out any thoughts of complaint or lack or annoyance and look towards what works, what's joyful, fun, exciting and new.

Make changes all the time to bring in the new.

Change the route to work if you can. If you always drive everywhere, try parking a little further away and walk a bit.

Change what you eat and drink. Go to bed earlier or later. Wake up earlier or later.

Change your room around. Move your bed to a different position in the room. Wear your 'best' clothes instead of saving them. Wear your hair a different way.

If you stay home a lot, go out a bit. If you go out a lot, stay home a bit.

Shuffle the energy up, discover something different all the time so that new energies and people can enter your world.

Just do it and watch the magic engage.

Every time you take one step towards something new and positive, the universe will take sixteen.

You won't be disappointed.

Daily affirmations, week 5

1

Focus on what you love in life
& more will come to love.

2

Love your life. It will start to move in the direction
of your dreams.

3

Love the people you live with. They will start to
please & delight you, or be replaced easily by
people who do.

4

Love where you live. You'll start to create the
home of your dreams.

5

Love your work. It will lead you
to your life purpose.

Your Weekly Wonder 5

If you have created a life that you are no longer wanting or perhaps have drawn in circumstances that are troubling you, remember it is your past thoughts that have set this up.

If you want to change your life, change your thinking right now, this second, to how you would like to feel and the world or set of circumstances you would like to be surrounding you. Stay only with these thoughts. Any time you revert to the mess around you, you are asking for more disruption to come in.

Focus all the time on the good you are wanting and how good you will feel when it is here. This will draw it to you, only this.

Your thoughts are all there is. They are drawing the essence of themselves to you right now.

The power to change anything is right here with us in our thoughts.

There is no reward and punishment system.

Our thoughts are alive, they go out into the ethers and draw circumstances to us that we are concentrating on.

Choose them wisely.

We can all choose a better life to live.

Which moment are you going to choose?

Daily affirmations, week 6

1

Be kind.

2

Develop the attitude of gratitude. Whenever you appreciate something, more rushes forward to be appreciated.

3

When you talk to others, look at them, listen to them. The way you treat others is the way you will be treated.

4

Whatever value you put on yourself, others will follow your lead.

5

No one is lesser than or better than, no matter how it seems.

Your Weekly Wonder 6

Your thoughts are all there is, drawing to you the essence of themselves right now.

The power to change anything is right here with us in our thoughts. What are yours drawing to you?

Is it what you want?

Thoughts are alive and draw circumstances to us. Use them wisely.

Most of us are giving to others more than we want to. We are in situations perhaps where people want more of us than we are willing to give.

People often say, "If you loved me, you would do this . . . ", "You are so mean" . . . or use many other ways of control . . . to get what they want from us.

"Be a good girl / boy and do this for me. You have to do this, you said you would . . . "

You are allowed to change your mind. You don't have to fit in all the time to please. We are just conditioned to. You are allowed to have a say and do what you want to do.

If you prefer to be at home, rather than be pushed out to be sociable because it suits your friends, you are allowed to. Work out what you want to do. You won't lose anyone because you prefer to do something different. You don't have to fit in to be liked.

Learn to say a big fat "no" sometimes . . . "This doesn't suit me just now." People won't like it at first, but they will soon begin to respect you more and you will draw people into your world who respect you, rather than take advantage of you. You will be happier doing more of what you want to do and be more fun to be around.

Wear what you want. Think what you want. Eat what you want. Do what you want. We are all different and everything is OK.

We don't have to fit in and do what others want from us . . . unless we choose to. There is so much pressure on being accepted and fitting in and being the same as everyone else, but we are all individuals. Our likes and dislikes are different. Do what you want to do. Make sure your needs are met first.

If you are continually putting others first, you will eventually explode and undo any good you have achieved. To remain calm under all circumstances your needs must be met. Your energy needs to be strong and full.

Pressure is fine occasionally, it helps keep us sharp, but continual pressure just like a pressure cooker has to be released, otherwise it will explode.

To have a calm harmonious life that works, put first what is important to you, even if it means others are annoyed that you are not doing what pleases them. You cannot people-please all the time: you would be ill.

Also, if you meet your needs yourself, you won't need to lean on others. If you are continually stretching yourself, this is the message you will give to others and they will ask more and more of you. Do what you want to do first and your life will be balanced, always.

We are all absolutely fine, more than fine, we are all perfect just the way we are, a spark of the divine, immortal, everlasting, eternal beings. We forget this. God did not make a mistake with us.

Have fun being you.

Perfect as you are.

Daily affirmations, week 7

1

Do what you love: the money will follow.

2

Whatever you wish you were doing is what you are supposed to be doing.

3

Follow your bliss.

4

There is always enough. Just because you have everything you want doesn't mean there's less for others. There's no limit.

5

Remember how magnificent you are. You are a co- creator with God. An eternal everlasting spark of the Divine.

Your Weekly Wonder 7

Whatever you want for yourself in life you have all the tools available at your fingertips this time round to achieve it.

There is nothing you cannot be, do or have. If you truly want it, you can have it, so long as you have no attachment to how it comes, from whom and from where.

If you can imagine something, you can have it. It is the universal law.

If you have dreams of being a musician, an entertainer, an artist, you have talents and gifts that you can develop to become what it is you would like to be.

If you wish to create buildings, bridges, road systems, you will have the necessary skills available within you to develop . . . If you wish to write or paint or cook or play football, tennis, rugby, swim, create gardens, jewellery, cars, boats or design wallpaper or aquariums, be a kindergarden teacher . . . you will have been born with the necessary talents and skills to accomplish whatever it is your heart desires.

You are never given a dream without the wherewithal to achieve it.

That's not to say it will necessarily come to you easily, you may have to work hard at it. But if it is what your heart tells you, you would like to do, your efforts towards it will be fun, not hard work, not a struggle.

If you are struggling, with anything, you are off track. Pull back to base and listen to your heart.

What would you love to be doing?

Do it lots.

This is your way forward. This is what you are supposed to be doing.

Something that makes your heart sing, something you would do all day whether you were paid or not. Pursue this in whatever way you can, even if it is only possible at first in between your "regular" work.

Opportunities will then present themselves to make it your life's work.

Don't hate the work you have. Find the good there even if it's only that it pays the rent.

You can never leave a situation you hate, it is tied to you by the law of attraction.

You need to find something good always in a situation, so that it brings more and more good to you and eventually anything that is not good has no place any longer in your life.

A new concept, but one that makes perfect sense once you start living it and let go of the old way of struggle.

Daily affirmations, week 8

1

Life is supposed to be fun:
you are meant to have a good time.
Do something today that brings you joy.

2

Clear the space you live in.
Your thoughts will be clearer.

3

Things you have around you are a reflection of
who you are. What do yours tell you about you?

4

Get rid of the old to make room for the new.

5

Only have things around you that uplift & make
you feel good.

Your Weekly Wonder 8

Only have objects, possessions around you that make you feel good.

Get rid of anything that saddens or annoys you, be it a mistaken clothes purchase, unwanted gift, someone else's choice of wallpaper, anything that when you look at it makes you feel bad. Try to donate or bin anything that causes your energy to drop when you look at it. Only have around you what is beautiful or really useful.

Often we live with a whole load of unwanted, unnecessary clutter. We defend our hoarding by explaining that it just may come in useful one day. Perhaps someone gave us a gift which we hate but feel we must keep for fear of causing offence. Let it go somewhere else, it doesn't mean that you don't appreciate the thought.

Often we have shelves filled with magazines and books we haven't read in years. Try to be really disciplined and throw away anything you haven't used or worn in the last couple of years. If you really cannot part with it, at least package it up and move it out of your living space for six months or so. If you still haven't needed it, bin or donate it somewhere. Your life will be so much freer and clearer and there will be a wonderful space for fresh ideas and experiences that there was perhaps no space for before.

You will feel healthier and younger in your clearer fresher space. You will be able to think more clearly and follow through with new ideas now there is space for them to manifest, be it a relationship or career or just fun new fresh 'stuff' that you actually use and enjoy.

Not having any clear space may be the only thing blocking a new relationship or career move.

Try it. It's pure magic. You will feel so light and airy.

Remember there are no mistakes. Life is always moving forward.

Anything you part with, if you really need it, will be replaced by its equivalent or something better, always.

It is the Law of the Universe.

Have fun.

Daily affirmations, week 9

1

Happiness is an inside job. Decide to be happy today no matter what is going on around you.

2

On waking, decide today is going to be a good day, full of wonderful surprises.

3

On waking, visualise today going really well, everything going your way.

4

Give something away, a smile, a compliment, a good wish.

5

Smile for no reason . . . . . it will bring something for you to smile about !!

Your Weekly Wonder 9

If you want to become a different person, fitter, richer, more successful, tidier, more organised, more elegant, more loved . . . .

You must become this new person ALL the time, ALL the time.

You can't just do it when it suits and conditions are right, or claim you will be this different person when the right conditions arrive; for example when your new partner, job, figure, house or car turns up. You have to be this new person now and behave as he or she would if the new conditions you are asking for were here.

The new conditions will be here once you let go the old conditions of them not being, because you will be on a vibration frequency that matches what you are looking for and now you will be allowing the new to step in.

You have to BE the change you are looking for, otherwise you will just attract the same old, same old.

Nothing will happen differently until you make changes in you, in the way you think and the way you behave, that attracts something different into your world.

You are the one in control.
No one is stopping you being, doing, having, except you, and the good news is that if you take just one tiny step towards the new, the universe will leap in with about 16 to help . . . but you must take that first one step in your thinking and change the frequency you are on to one of allowing all good things to happen, by becoming that change that you are asking for.

Daily affirmations, week 10

1

Choose to see the good today: it's always there.

2

Always go the extra mile . . . give that little bit of extra service, a little more courtesy, make someones' day. Like a boomerang it will return.

3

Try not to judge . . . . . you'll draw judgement to you from others.

4

When you criticize anything ask yourself, "where do I do that?" . . . . .

5

Stay away from people who make you feel bad.

Your Weekly Wonder 10

The more difficult a person is being, whether he is a child or an adult, the more love he needs. He is just asking for more of your love & is wanting you to take more notice, so that he feels appreciated. All of us just want to be loved. No one means to be difficult.

The more difficult people become, the more they need your love & acceptance, not your anger & criticism.

Try & look deeper & see what is really happening for them. You will then be part of the solution not the problem.

This doesn't mean you have to condone bad behaviour, it means you don't add to the problem by taking offence and fighting back, making it personal & taking it as an attack on you.

Taking offence is as bad as giving offence.

If you can be the one who remains calm, being understanding & kind, reassuring the other person you are willing to listen & try to understand what is troubling them with no judgement, you can diffuse the situation.

It is only when you fight back, taking it personally, that the situation gets out of hand.

Be the change you want.
If you want a peaceful life,
Be peaceful.

Daily affirmations, week 11

1

*If life's not working, change your thoughts. If you
keep thinking the same things,
you'll get the same results.*

2

*Your job is to know what you want.
How it comes to you is the universe's job.*

3

*Live in any small way you can,
as you will when you have what you want.*

4

*Are you ready & willing to receive what you are
asking for? Are you sure?*

5

*Be the change that you want.
Be ready for it when it comes.*

Your Weekly Wonder 11

Be what it is that you are wanting to attract into your life.

To have changes in your life you must be living on the same vibrational frequency as your desire for it to come to you.

You need to live as though what you are asking for is already here.

Then it can come to you and you will recognise it.

If you want to attract romance into your world but all you do is complain about how lonely you are and relationships never work for you, guess what? You'll get more of that, but . . .

If you begin to notice happy couples having fun together and think "yep I'll have some of that, thats for me," and start appreciating all the good stuff you already have in your life to date, your new love will just drift in. . . because you are now on a frequency of receiving.

Same with wanting more money or a new career.

Spend time only appreciating what you have already and noticing things that you would like in a "wouldn't it be nice if I had that" way.

See things you would like to buy and think, "yes, that's for me." Notice people who love their work and are successful and say, "yes, that's for me."

It will all start to come towards you because now you are starting to concentrate more on what you do want rather than what you don't.

The universe doesn't know the difference between positive and negative, lack or abundance. You will just draw to you more of what you are thinking about.

Make sure it's more of what you want.

Daily affirmations, week 12

1

You can have anything you can imagine having, but you have to believe you can & act accordingly.

2

If you see a quality in a person that you admire, you have that quality, otherwise you wouldn't recognise it.

3

Be pleased when others are successful, say, "well done" & think, "that's for me", "I'll have that too." There are no limits.

4

Give freely, don't hoard anything. Whatever you give out you'll get back a hundred times.

5

Save, but don't save for a "rainy" day, the "rainy" day will definitely come if you are expecting it !!

Your Weekly Wonder 12

This manifestation stuff is not as simple as it sounds.

What does it mean being on the same vibrational frequency as the thing you are wanting?

Living as if you have already got it for it to come in?

It seems again to be a paradox, like all this spiritual knowledge. You seem to need no attachment at all to what you are wanting and at the same time a strong, non-negotiable 'this just has to happen' attitude.

Anything in between seems to smack of lack and it doesn't come.

I think as most of the books say on this subject, forget the thinking, requesting, asking for.

Live as though you have a written guarantee that whatever you want is on its way.
You no longer have to think about 'how'.
It's a done deal.

You would act, live and be in a very different

way if you were certain it was on its way. You would be living as though you already had it because you have !

This is the vibe we need to be on to draw in whatever we want. The certainty that it is ours. We don't have to earn it or be worthy of it or worry whether we are asking too much. It is just ours. Whatever it is, so long as we can imagine having it, it is ours. No question about it: so long as it is not a specific person or it belongs to someone else, you are asking for what is yours. The same as they have perhaps, its equivalent or something better.

We need to feel with absolute certainty it is there for us, just as we would if we had a guarantee. This eliminates the attachment to 'having to have' because it is ours.

I think this is what enables us to live with the mindset necessary to draw in what we want instantly.

Anything else means we are wanting, which equals waiting.

Daily affirmations, week 13

1

The universe doesn't hear the difference between a negative or a positive: it will give you what you are thinking, good or bad !!

2

The universe doesn't see the difference between fantasy and reality. Imagine it: you can have it.

3

Stay calm. Eventually, everything passes. Good is always on its way.

4

Sometimes it's harder to stay with a situation than it is to change it.

5

Change is good.

Your Weekly Wonder 13

People react to us mostly the way we expect them to. If you want people to react to you differently, start telling a better-feeling story to yourself about your life and how people react to you.

We get only what we think about and if we change our thinking to what we want rather than what we don't, the results can be instantaneous.

So start imagining that you've got that job, or that special person does answer the phone.

You may or may not get that exact job or the exact person answering the phone, but what you will get is the equivalent or something better, whatever is perfect for you.

It is difficult to make changes, but if we keep functioning in the same way day after day, we will only get the same results: fine if life is working well for us, but if you want changes, try and change your expectations of situations and people to good ones.

Start relating only the good experiences you have and good things that happen to you; talk mostly about those and watch your world change. . .

You won't ever go back.

Daily affirmations, week 14

1

*If you are unsure which direction to go,
do nothing.*

2

*If you have to make a decision, take the issue to
your heart. What feels best?*

3

*Once you have made a decision, put all your
energy into that. Don't ever look back.*

4

*Everything is always good & moving us in the
direction we want to go the fastest way possible.*

5

*There are no mistakes.
Mistakes are shortcuts in disguise.*

Your Weekly Wonder 14

Take stock of what is and is not working in your life and look at – if not, why not?

If you have a dream or a wish that is not falling into place, the only thing stopping it is you.

Look to see where you are blocking it.

For example, say it's more money you are interested in, perhaps you have a belief you need to change that tells you money is hard to come by.

Money is only for a select few.

Money is easy come easy go, slips through your fingers. You have to work hard to achieve anything.

Life is all work and no play.

Work out what beliefs are stopping you having what you want.

Start to say, I now have more money than I can possibly use. Money comes to money. I do what I love and the money follows. Work is play and play is work.There is more than enough for everyone. Everything I touch turns to gold.

Use whatever words work for you, create your own new belief system and completely erase the old ones that are no longer serving you.

Once you change your belief system, start showing active faith that money is on its way, by for example, always carrying notes in your wallet, notes will always make you feel good. Always keep your petrol tank over half full, this will also make you feel richer and more abundant.

Whatever it is you want, be it changes in health, career, relationship, finance – as soon as you work out where your thoughts are blocking you on the subject and you see what changes in your belief system you need to make, and put the new belief system into practice, change will start to come immediately.

When you make changes in any area of your life, it has a knock-on effect to other areas, as everything is connected, so once you start to change your belief system, the better it gets, the better it gets.

So set yourself free. Stop blaming anyone else for holding you back.

Use your power and start to create a life you love by changing the way you think. Thoughts are everything. That is all you need to do. Things will then start to fall into place.

The fast forward button is how quickly you are able to adjust to your new beliefs.

Have fun.

Daily affirmations, week 15

1

You have everything you need to succeed.

2

Ask & it will be given, knock & it will be opened.
You are never alone.

3

Pick yourself up & start again.
There is no other way.

4

Find something to be grateful for.

5

See the good. The rest will fall away.

Your Weekly Wonder 15

Today I concentrate on feeling good. Whatever I look at I enjoy and see only good.

My body responds by relaxing and every single cell plumps up, renews, rejuvenates and restores.

I realise feeling good is the secret to looking good, the secret to youthful, beautiful, serene, relaxed looks.

I am going to do it lots.

All of me relaxes and responds to these beautiful, calm, good feelings.

I realise feeling good is the secret to looking good. All of me responds with glowing positive health.

I will concentrate on that which feels good, always.

Daily affirmations, week 16

1

In yourself, notice only the good.

2

Compliment yourself.

3

Allow yourself to be as you would like to be.

4

Do only what you choose to do.

5

*If you have to do something you don't like,
change your attitude towards it.*

Your Weekly Wonder 16

Realise we are all doing the best we can with the knowledge we have. Everyone is only trying to be happier.

Being happier is the desire behind anything we wish to draw into our world. We believe the having of it will make us happy, but how often have we got exactly what we wanted and found it didn't make us happy for very long? We began to crave the next house, job, person, gizmo.

Happiness is an inside job. We have to make a decision to be happy, it doesn't come from anything outside of us.

When we find happiness, just because we decide to focus and choose to concentrate on things we see that please us, rather than the opposite, we can start to live happily and stop our search outside of ourself. Then anything that comes in extra is icing on the cake.

Daily affirmations, week 17

1

*Today, try to please yourself
more than you please others.*

2

Put yourself first.

3

*In any situation, ask: "am I reacting to this out of
love or fear?" Choose love.*

4

*In any situation, ask:
"how can I be more loving here?"*

5

*When you are doing things you want to do
you will do them well.*

Your Weekly Wonder 17

Notice how others treat you. It is a reflection of how you treat yourself. If you want better treatment from others, start to think of yourself and what you do in a better light. Others will follow your lead.

Treat other people the way you would like to be treated.

Do you want to be criticised, shown a "better way" to do something, told what is wrong, what needs fixing, what and how you should say something etc, etc?

I don't think so !

We are all doing the best we can with the knowledge we have.

Criticism doesn't help at all, it just pushes people away or at best chips away at the love they have for us.

Praise helps, always, and brings people closer.

It's what you want isn't it?

Give it to them,

All of them.

Be the change you want.

As with everything, like a boomerang, it will return to you.

Daily affirmations, week 18

1

*What would you love to do whether you were paid
or not? Try to move towards this.
It is your life purpose.*

2

*Try only to spend time with
people you love being with.*

3

*Try to do things you love to do. If you have
forgotten, try everything until you find something,
then do it lots.*

4

Make a decision to be happy.

5

Your happiness will lift & inspire others.

Your Weekly Wonder 18

Do what you love and the money will follow. Try to stay away from what you feel you 'ought' to do. Do what you love, you will put your heart and soul into it and love every minute.

We spend a third of our day working. It's good to love and look forward to that time, not just survive and get through our nine to five, looking forward only to our evenings, weekends and couple of weeks' holiday a year.

We all have something that we love to do. We are all good and able to shine at something. Perhaps your dreams are so hidden and tucked away that you have forgotten what you love to do.

What were you good at at school? What did you love to do hobby-wise? What did you used to do as a child, teenager, where time just disappeared, you were so happy doing what you loved?

What would you do all day, every day now if you didn't have to earn a living? That is what you need to do, that is your life purpose, that is where your energy needs to go.

Don't worry too much about 'earning' a living. When you start to love what you do, the money will just flow. Obviously until you get into this way of thinking you will need to keep your present mode of earning your keep, but if you find something, anything, to appreciate from what you do at the moment, even if it is only that it pays the rent until the change comes, it will speed the process along.

Appreciation brings more in to appreciate.

When you do what you love, everything falls into place in life, because you are concentrating on fun, more comes in to enjoy because you get more of what you are thinking.

This is how life works.

The only reason any of us don't have what we want from life are all those thoughts we have about our life not working.

So when we are thinking about how good our day is and how much we are enjoying whatever it is that makes our hearts sing, more of it will come in, and more, and more.

This is the secret. Do what you love and the money follows.

Daily affirmations, week 19

1

Honour yourself.
Always present yourself the best you can.

2

Create a wonderful living space for yourself.
Clear the clutter & clean everything.

3

Make time for yourself.

4

Eat healthily, honour your body
by feeding it nourishing foods.

5

Relax more, sleep more if you need to.

Your Weekly Wonder 19

Your living conditions are a reflection of you.

How does your personal space look? Is it clear, clean, fresh, up to the minute? Or is it cluttered, dusty, a bit stuck, stacked with stuff?

Clear what you no longer use or wear, clean everything up, inject new fresh energy into it.

Fix whatever is broken, in need of repair. Try not to have broken equipment around you, it tends to slow you down. If everything is kept up to date, your requests are delivered more quickly because you have thrown forward the energy of how you like things done immediately and the universe will follow your lead and deliver your dreams and requests instantly.

So get sorting, fixing. Not only will you feel clearer and brighter, you will be more organised, get more done in a shorter space of time. You'll be able to put your hand on what you need immediately without wading through stuff trying to remember where you put the keys, small change for the car park, dog's lead etc.

Your energy levels and health will improve as you start to clear. You'll have a lot more energy to start new projects and make changes.

Everything is a reflection of you.

How is your space looking?

Great?

Thought so . . .

Daily affirmations, week 20

1

Do only what needs to be done today. Don't stress yourself with everything, just handle today.

2

Find time today for you. Turn everything off. Just be by yourself, even for ten minutes. Listen to the silence.

3

Make spaces in between the tasks, to notice the sky, the sunshine, the quiet.

4

Be kind to yourself, have a break, find the stillness, even if only for a few minutes.

5

Take a 'power nap' even if it's only for ten minutes, enjoy the stillness, re-charge.

Your Weekly Wonder 20

Sometimes we are overwhelmed with circumstances in our life that have got a little out of hand because we have been condoning bad behaviour in one way or another, either in the work place or with friendships or relationships.

Clear out the dross in all sorts of areas, practical, physical, emotional, and let go of anything that is no longer serving you.

You may find yourself moving away from people you used to be friends with, changing your area of work, clearing out cupboards, garages, loft space, any area that is stuck or clogged, not only in your home and surroundings but also in your way of thinking and behaving. Have no fear of anything or anyone leaving during these changes. We cannot lose anything that is 'meant' for us: people, circumstances will either change to fit our new ideas of life or disappear painlessly and we'll no longer want or need them.

Also your tolerance levels will change, you will feel more definite about what you will and will not put up with in your daily life.

You will feel drawn to creating more harmony and to access harmony we need peace of mind and peace of heart in all areas, which means change.

Change is always good. What do you plan to change? Start now. Be part of the solution.

Choose harmony in yourself, your relationships, your surroundings.

Get clearing !!

Daily affirmations, week 21

1

Re-invent yourself, go for the best you can be.

2

Revamp your space, make it fit who you are now.

3

Re-charge your batteries, you're worth it.

4

Restore order in your world,
sort anything that needs attention.

5

Spend time daydreaming,
you're creating your future.

Your Weekly Wonder 21

Be clear who you are. Honour yourself. Be a clear shiny light. Work on yourself so this is so. Know you are a powerful magnetic being. Realise we don't get what we want, we get what we are.

What we are thinking about and concentrating on we get more of. This is the law. Remember your thoughts are the building blocks, they go out into the ethers and create your tomorrow.

Monitor what you are thinking for a while, every half hour or so. Check that your thoughts are on track, creating what you want and not, as often is the case, the opposite.

Set big goals for yourself; aim high. Goals that make you want to get out of bed in the mornings to get started.

Declutter objects and people that need to be released from your life to give you a clear canvas to work on.

Listen always to your intuition. Ask for signs if you don't notice any. You will be shown clearly, if you ask, there is always an answer to every question and once you start tuning in you will see the answer is usually part of the question.

Have a hobby. Do more of what you love and the money will follow.

Look after yourself. Be reliant on yourself. Trust the universe: it will take care of you. You cannot help others until you are balanced and totally secure in yourself.

Daily affirmations, week 22

1

*Ask for every single cell of your body to be
restored to the blueprint of perfection.*

2

Expect a miracle.

3

*See yourself as you would like to be every time you
pass a mirror.*

4

*Recharge your batteries
by doing something you love.*

5

*Find love & enthusiasm for things, dance through
life on happy feet, fake it until it arrives,
it has to arrive !!*

Your Weekly Wonder 22

Life is full of wonderful surprises. The more we realise and notice this the more magic appears in our day to day.

Whatever we are appreciating and concentrating on grows, so the better it gets, the better it gets.

Whenever you feel a little unsure or lost, look around for something to appreciate and enjoy, break the spell quickly, find something good to concentrate on and more will come into your world to appreciate.

Be ever vigilant to stay on the side of having and enjoying.

It's hard work at first, but it will become a habit you will be unable to break as you see your life continue to improve for the good.

Daily affirmations, week 23

1

To take offence is as bad as to give offence.

2

*Give something to everyone you meet today,
even if it's only a smile or a compliment
or to wish them well.*

3

Be the first to smile, to say, 'hello'.

4

Make everyone's day better for having met you.

5

Remember to say 'thank you'.

Your Weekly Wonder 23

Sometimes there seems to be a reverence about the world, as though the world has been washed.

Take note and look with new eyes, new expectations. Feel the energy of the new vibration as it cushions you and heals your frantic thoughts and fears.

Feel the calmness that engulfs the world.

You who are open and and aware of spirit will feel the calmness wash you leaving you rejuvenated and whole.

Can you feel the peace in the air? Can you feel the new vibration filtering through? Have you noticed everything is calmer and less fraught, there is a smoothness to everything where there were once jagged edges.

Can you feel the new vibration? Notice how confident and alive you feel, how aware you can become.

Bathe in the serenity and love that the vibration promises and emerge at peace. A peace that others will see and wish to emulate.

All the talking in the world will not have the same effect as seeing a face relaxed and at peace with itself and life.

This is the way. Live in a way that displays how a life is guided by spirit for good.

Daily affirmations, week 24

1

Bring the mountain to the market place.

2

Trust in God but tie your camel to a tree.

3

*You'll never get to enlightenment by the caravan
of thinking, you have to feel your way.*

4

*Any course of action you take, take to your heart,
does it feel good, how does it feel?
Your body will tell you.*

5

*You don't have to fight, you don't have to win,
you just have to know.*

Your Weekly Wonder 24

*Our old ways are no longer working. We are all
divorcing ourselves from situations that are no
longer serving us and can be or have been quite
damaging to us. Whether this be in the ways we
are thinking or actual communication with others,
all of us are receiving strength and new insights
empowering us in greater and deeper ways to
enable an escape.*

*Try and make notes of any dreams, visions,
insights that may help you move forwards,
otherwise they tend to disappear into nothing and
you forget you've even had them.*

*Keep them alive by paying attention to them.
We are moving towards bravery, to make changes
where, before, we may have held back through
fear of disrupting relationships or risking
someones' displeasure. We are becoming
increasingly influenced by our gut reactions, less
by our mind telling us what is appropriate.*

*Past situations are returning, reminding us
what we definitely do not want, and this helps us
get clear on what we do want. It is only when we
are pushed to our farthest limit that we reach our
personal boundaries and are finally able to say,
"no, this far and no further". Only then are we
able to say "yes" to what we do want.*

It is often only when we see what we do not

want that what we do want becomes perfectly clear.

With this increased bravery comes a surge of energy to help propel us forward in whatever direction we feel led.

We know where we want to go.

Now is the time for honest relaxation, a true balance between being and doing, co-operation and competition, feeling and thinking.

Gently and firmly empower yourself.

All external impressions have been replaced; it's now all to do with inner space and peace.

Daily affirmations, week 25

1

How long are you going to remain stuck?

2

How long are you going to blame others for where you are?

3

If you continue doing what you are doing, how will your life look in 5 years' time? Will you have what you want?

4

You need to BE the change that you want.

5

It is really hard work to be happy, it takes real discipline, but it is worth it.

Your Weekly Wonder 25

The best thing you can do for yourself is dream about your future. Imagine it in your mind's eye in every detail that you can. Imagine how overjoyed and blown away you will be on its arrival.

This is more powerful than all the action in the world that you yourself could take to make it happen. It's the universe's job to show you what action you take.

Your job is to dream and imagine how you will feel when everything you want is here.

When you can truly feel the excitement and joy, whatever you have asked for will jump towards you like pins to a magnet. It is the law. What action you need to take will appear as a natural joyful next step.

The only things that will delay your dream are your thoughts against it: "it's too good to be true", "it can never happen to me", "it's only a dream", etc . . . Don't give these thoughts house room.

Just keep believing in your dream and dream

more.

It's not about deciding what action to take. The action part, the steps in between, the "how" it will all come about is not your job.

You'll be blown away by a plan offered from the universe. It will be far better than you would ever have thought of.

Your job is only to imagine and get clear on all that you would like to be, do and have. It's all about dreaming, imagining, visualising, living "as if".

The action to take will come about as a natural fun next step.

Don't get hung up on the action, just keep dreaming.

Daily affirmations, week 26

1

Anything you are nervous about – a romantic meeting, job interview, dentist's appointment – imagine the outcome you want before you go & watch the magic.

2

A happy person never got sick.

3

You have a duty to yourself to do what you want to do & remain well.

4

Live life, dance more, sing more, smile more, have fun.

5

Daydream more. If you can imagine it, you can have it.

Your Weekly Wonder 26

If you don't feel good, you are contradicting your thoughts: wanting something, then telling yourself you cannot have it, you don't deserve it, that there is no way you can make it happen, and so on.

Yes there is.

Life is supposed to be fun, joyful, feel like a wonderful game, "I want it, I get it. I want it, I get it. I want it, I get it."

It's all about fun, creating and having. The only thing that stops us creating what we want are the thoughts that we have against us having it.

Your feelings tell you how well you are doing, how close you are to your goals.

If you feel great you are well on track. If you feel less than great you are contradicting your wants somewhere and working against yourself. So all the time you are calling to you what you want, but just before it arrives pushing it away by convincing yourself it feels too good to be true, you're expecting or asking for far too much, or whatever thoughts you choose. Nothing is too good to be true, nothing is too wonderful to happen. Nothing is too much to ask.

Just envisage what you want and know you are worth it and it is on its way . . . start allowing it to come all the way to you.

Daily affirmations, week 27

1

Say, 'only right action is taking place in my life.'

2

I am a magnet for my good.

3

Life is full of wonderful surprises.

4

I only think good, see good, speak good.
There is no end to my good.

5

Today is a day of balance.
Only good comes to me.

Your Weekly Wonder 27

Be kinder to yourself. Love yourself more. Treat yourself in a better way. Others take their cue from you on the way you would like to be treated by the way you treat yourself.

So if others are treating you unkindly or you feel, "less than", up your thoughts to good ones about everything you do. Then so will everyone else and you'll be a lot happier.

Give to yourself first what you would like from others and watch them follow your lead.

Have fun with it.

See that you are the only power in your universe and you can change anything just by thinking about it differently.

Use life as a mirror more, to see where you need to make changes.

Daily affirmations, week 28

1

Only divine right action is taking place in my life.

2

Today I am going to be the best I can be.

3

Today I am a magnet for my good.

4

Only good things come to me.

5

My life is full of wonderful surprises.

Your Weekly Wonder 28

The good thing about people opposing us and it troubling us is that we are given a gift here. When they go against us, or do something we don't agree with or something that doesn't sit well with us – in that moment the solution, the opposite of what they are doing, the thing we do want, comes into being very clearly as we focus on it. And so what we do want is given birth in that moment and shoots out to come into being.

So even situations we don't like are good because they help us to see the opposite of them, what we do want, and this sets it into motion to come to us.

Win, win.

Daily affirmations, week 29

1

I look for the good in everything,
knowing that, as I look, I shall find.

2

I see the good in everyone. I know it is there.

3

I salute the divinity in everyone,
instead of being judgemental.

4

I cease having to be right;
I consider another point of view.

5

I choose happiness over making my point.

Your Weekly Wonder 29

*Are you giving the right message to the universe?
Are you living in the moment? Are all your tasks
completed? Up to date? Do you leave stuff
unfinished? Are you spending time with people
whom you love and who love you? Do you always
present yourself in the best way you can? Are
your living conditions well cared for? Do you feed
yourself nourishing foods and look after yourself?*

*Show the universe you are serious about
having a fantastic life by making the life you have
created at the moment as good as you can.*

*If you are not orderly, you'll draw in more
disorder. If you are "making do", you'll draw in
more areas where you have to "make do".*

*If you are tidy and up to date with day to day
maintenance around you, more order will come
into every area of your life. If you are calm and
tranquil you'll get more harmony flowing to you
in all areas.*

*If you are up to date with your tasks and
complete projects, the universe will be up to date
with your requests because the message you will
be giving is one of immediate completion.*

*You must give the right message and live as
much as you can under the circumstances you
have now, just as you will when you receive what
it is you are asking for.*

This is your fast forward button.

Daily affirmations, week 30

1

I let life be a deep "let go", cease being in control and watch the magic.

2

I trust that I will be led to the next step.

3

I trust that what I need will be placed in front of me at the exact moment.

4

I realise on this pathway I will only be able to see one step at a time, not the whole plan.

5

I trust that there is a plan and all I have to do is go with what is in front of me, having only the end result in mind.

Your Weekly Wonder 30

It doesn't matter where we have come from, what's happened to us thus far.

All that matters is that we now have easier access to how the universe works than ever before. All the information, once hidden, is now easily available for us to study and learn from.

The basics are simple. Life is meant to be fun and joyful and we create our reality as we go by our thoughts and feelings.

No fate, no destiny, no reward and punishment system. Just us creating as we go, all the time, from our thoughts, and the universe giving to us what we are thinking about and concentrating on the most.

Start with baby steps if you like, thinking and manifesting small things: maybe for example a car parking space or a small amount of extra money, or think big and have it all immediately, your choice. Play with it. Life is your play ground. You have all the power to be, do, or have whatever you would like. Use it.

Daily affirmations, week 31

1

*I see joy and beauty all around,
realising that, by noticing it, I am creating more.*

2

*I fill my life with beauty and order wherever I can,
knowing the order and beauty will overflow into
areas that are chaotic.*

3

*I become the best I can be and remain calm in all
situations, knowing there are no mistakes and all
is leading towards my good.*

4

*Today I am an example to others that I can
achieve anything I wish in life.*

5

*I create balance in my life by concentrating only
on what is good.*

Your Weekly Wonder 31

Life is all about fun, joy and having. How much fun are you having? Have you forgotten how it works? Wake up and start enjoying life. You have the power to turn your world round in any moment you choose and have the life you want, just by changing the way you think and therefore drawing what you most want to you, even if you don't know what you want.

Knowing what you don't want is a good starting point because you want the opposite. Start there, play with it, expand on it, dream about having it, dream of it all taking shape and coming into being.

Imagine how life would be, how you would feel. You are on your way.

Daily affirmations, week 32

1

*Life is always good and moving me in the
direction I want to go, even if I can't always see it.*

2

*Whatever is happening is moving me in the
direction of my good, even if it moves opposite to
what I think I want.*

3

Life is full of surprises, all of them good.

4

*Whenever something doesn't work out I look for
the good & know there is a better way being found.*

5

*Whenever something doesn't work out in the time I
have in mind I know it is only a delay, not a
denial. I know it will come.*

Your Weekly Wonder 32

The most important thing in life is that you feel good. All the time.

All the time, no matter what is happening. Do whatever it takes. When you feel good you are on the vibration of receiving all good things because like attracts like. Therefore if you are happy and feel good, more good is being drawn to you all the time. Other stuff will come in as well but if you are disciplined and make sure you concentrate, notice only the good, the rest will fall away.

The secret is to concentrate on the good stuff above all else. The more you notice and appreciate the good, the more your life will touch on bliss and the rest will just fall away . . . because you give it no attention, therefore you give it no life and it just disappears.

Daily affirmations, week 33

1

In difficult circumstances, try to change your attitude. Either the situation or person will change, or something better will replace it.

2

When people are being difficult, before you react, try to open your heart one more notch and see what they are afraid of.

3

Try not to judge. "You don't know anyone," the old saying says, "until you have walked ten miles in his moccasins."

4

Even seeming mistakes have a good outcome, always.

5

Life is always moving in the direction of your good, even if it doesn't always seem to be.

Your Weekly Wonder 33

*Every time you see your reflection in the mirror,
thank yourself for turning up and just being you.
Think of how much time and care you have put
into you thus far.*

*How many times have you chosen and
prepared food to nourish yourself, bathed, washed
your hair, brushed your teeth, clothed, exercised,
entertained yourself? How much time have you
put into practising your creative skills? How
much effort have you put into making friendships
to help you thrive? Thank and appreciate yourself
for doing all of this for you.*

*Thank yourself for turning up and keeping on
when life has been hard. Tell yourself how much
you appreciate your bravery and effort.*

*Compliment yourself on where you have done
really well in any competitions or exams you have
taken or when you have completed something.*

*Start to be your own best friend and appreciate
yourself, all the time.*

*No more criticizing, accusing or telling
yourself what you didn't do. Only have*

appreciation and love for yourself, and all that you have accomplished and achieved in your life this far.

Your life will become magical and you will blossom once you feed yourself love and appreciation, and the big plus is others will start to treat you this way too.

We give others their cue on how to treat us by the way we treat ourselves. They follow our lead.

Make sure your lead is all love and appreciation for you.

Daily affirmations, week 34

1

You are always OK in the present moment.

2

*If this moment is OK,
the rest of your life will be OK.*

3

*Trust that you are being taken care of
and that all is well.*

4

*Everything is always perfectly perfect.
Without the odd hiccup you may not know clearly
what you want.*

5

*Focus on the good; the rest will fall away.
It takes discipline but is essential for creating an
exceptionally successful life.*

Your Weekly Wonder 34

Be kinder to yourself. Make yourself right more.
Praise yourself. Thank yourself for the way you look after yourself on a daily basis. Start to be your own best friend.
See yourself as doing a good job always, the best you can. Make a list of everything you do for others, how you take care of them, treat them. Do the same for yourself.
Put yourself at the top of the list and ask, "what would I like to do?" Not "what should I do, what needs to be done?" but "what would be fun?" Do that first.
You will find when you are happy all that "needs" to be done falls into place and is taken care of easily because you are coming from a happier, more joyful starting point.

Daily affirmations, week 35

1

*If anything saddens or upsets you, you're
misunderstanding something really important.*

2

If it hurts, it's not love.

3

*Whatever you notice in another,
you do somewhere.*

4

*If something doesn't work out,
trust a better way is being found.*

5

*You have all you need to succeed
this lifetime round.*

Your Weekly Wonder 35

When something appears to be a hassle or difficult to do, pull back and, every time you think of it, thank the universe that it is done. Imagine it finished, see the end result in your mind's eye, then do something else, take your mind off it. You will find when the time comes to do it, it is sorted easily, even if it is you who has to do it: it won't be difficult because you have already visualised it completed. Change your attitude and everything becomes easier to accomplish.

We are often getting in our own way by deciding, "life is hard", "I can't do that ", "people are always difficult". Change your thoughts to "everything is easy", " people are easy to get along with", "life is fun".

Watch the magic.

Daily affirmations, week 36

1

If something leaves your life, even if you push it away, it will always be replaced by something better.

2

Trust the process of life to bring you what you want.

3

Your first thought on any situation is always the "right" one; then come the doubts. Go with the first one.

4

Flee from anything that flees from thee.

5

What if everything that is happening right now is a good thing, leading you to where you want to go?

Your Weekly Wonder 36

Start to get to know yourself. Find out what you like. What do you love doing? What would you do all day every day whether you were paid or not? What foods do you like? What sort of weather do you like?

Do you like to walk, run, play soccer, dance? Get to know yourself.

Start to see yourself as you would a new best friend. Ask yourself the questions you would ask him/her.

Who are you? What are your likes, dislikes, dreams, ambitions?

Make lists of what you have achieved so far. How well you have done.

If you can't think of many good things about yourself, recall times when you have noticed good qualities in others and know that you have these qualities yourself, otherwise you wouldn't recognise them in others.

Start to think about yourself in ways that encourage you, put yourself first, make yourself right.

This is not what we are taught as children: a new way of thinking.

If you are happy, everyone around you will be happier, like attracts like.

Daily affirmations, week 37

1

No one means any harm. Everyone is doing the best they can with the knowledge they have.

2

*Guilt and worry are a waste of time,
useless emotions: let them go.
Forgive yourself, forgive others, move on.*

3

Everyone wants to be loved.

4

Anything can be healed.

5

Be the change you want. If you want love, give it.

Your Weekly Wonder 37

Is your life going the way that you want it to go or just 'randomly' happening because you are not paying attention to your thoughts?

Take stock daily, turn everything round that is not what you want.

Are you waiting for a person, job, house move, opportunity to step in?

Check everything is up to date in your day to day, for example, do you pay your bills on time or are you always last minute? Do you fix anything that breaks at once or leave it until it 'has' to be done?

Do you return phone calls, send thank you notes, or is it all a bit hit and miss?

Start to get up to date with everything: dental appointments, to-do lists, everything. Show the universe you mean business by doing what ever needs to be fixed, sorted, paid at once. No delay or messing about. Then whenever you have a dream or desire, it is able to come to you more quickly because you have shown the universe that this is how you work and how you expect the universe to work; and it will, because that is now the vibration you are working on, immediate completion.

Daily affirmations, week 38

1

Anyone who is continually criticizing in a relationship, doesn't want the relationship.

2

If something is missing from a situation, it's what you're not putting in.

3

Work on yourself; don't try to control another's behaviour.

4

Be an example to others of what you want. If you want love, give love; if you want money, give some away; if you want to be a success, help others be successful.

5

Be the change you want. Live as though it's already here.

Your Weekly Wonder 38

*Do you surround yourself with people you love,
who love you, people you want to spend time with?*

*How much time are you spending doing what
you feel you ought to do rather than what you
want to do?*

*Talking to people you ought to talk to or spend
time with?*

*Do you have to avoid many people, phone
calls, invitations?*

*Are a lot of your friendships old ones that may
not be serving you any longer?*

*Is it time to let some things go to make space
for the glorious new?*

*It is important for your happiness to know
who you are and how you function, and whether
the way you work suits you or not and if it brings
the best to you.*

*Only you know and you know by the way
things make you feel.*

*Check in with your feelings, ask "how does this
person, activity, thought, make me feel?"*

*Simple as. If it feels good, do it; if it doesn't
don't . . . always go with the best-feeling thought.*

*It will be best for you and best for all
concerned.*

Daily affirmations, week 39

1

When you wake, decide this is a good day and all will go well. Hold a vision of the day going well.

2

Say, "All is easy to accomplish."

3

Only do things you feel good about doing. It will take half the time and be done twice as well.

4

If you have to do something you don't like, change your attitude.

5

There is always something good if you look for it.

Your Weekly Wonder 39

We are told money is one of the easiest things to manifest. If you find it difficult to imagine money just coming to you, perhaps try this idea. Make a list of what you think the universe could owe you for all the time you have put in up to now in helping others: for example counselling, babysitting, cooking, cleaning, repairing cars, decorating, cutting lawns, household repairs, gardening, sewing, running errands etc. etc.

Over the years it will come to quite a lot. Work out a sum you feel happy and comfortable to accept and write a cheque to yourself for this amount. If the amount seems too huge for you to accept, break it down into a series of smaller ones.

Put your cheque or cheques somewhere where you can easily see them. Each time you notice them it will remind you the money is on its way.

Every time you notice the cheque, say thank you, showing active faith in advance for the money you know is coming to you.

It will not necessarily appear in a way you expect, but the amount will start to trickle or rush to you, as with all things, depending on the amount of faith you have in your request manifesting.

Good Luck.

Daily affirmations, week 40

1

We are all connected. As you stretch and grow spiritually, it lifts everyone.

2

Nothing exists except now. Spend no time on regrets, forgive yourself, move on.

3

Only look backwards to see how far you have come, what good you have achieved.

4

Make the most of today. Do what you can. Whatever is left over is not today's job. It belongs to tomorrow and can wait.

5

Life is full of wonderful surprises. Say, "I am a magnet for my good."

Your Weekly Wonder 40

Try to be kind. You have no idea how your actions may affect another person. Try always to be understanding of another's viewpoint. There isn't ever only one answer to a situation. Everyone has a different opinion, a different angle. Ours isn't the only one or necessarily the right one; everyone has a point from where they are standing concerning what they see. We have no idea how our actions may affect other people.

To one person, criticism which might mean nothing to another could send them scuttling home to safety.

We don't know another's history, their past experiences, how they have been treated as a child or what issues they are dealing with. We don't know how our comments may affect them. The basic message is just be kind.

Think kind, be kind, act kind always. Treat others as you would like to be treated.

No one ever means any harm, it is just their way of asking for more love. The more difficult a person is being, the more they are asking for our love in the only way they know how.

Daily affirmations, week 41

1

Be ever vigilant with your thoughts. Spend time thinking <u>only</u> of what you want to happen.

2

Are you really excited & expectant of your new desired future?

Or still caught up in the same old, same old??

3

Nothing can ever change until you stop thinking & giving energy to what you <u>don't</u> want.

4

Concentrate only on what you <u>do</u> want, the rest will drop away.

5

Become the change you want in your behaviour & reactions. The material circumstances <u>will</u> follow.

Your Weekly Wonder 41

Sometimes we step into a slipstream and can enjoy the ride blessed with grace and harmony. A very different vibration from the one we had been experiencing previously.

We work out over these difficult times where our personal boundaries are, what we will and will not put up with, and hopefully all gain a value of ourselves that others can now respect and follow.

In this ascension time, harmony and peace are in reach. A calmer time ahead is offered, all to do with honour of self. Once we respect ourselves, only then can others respect us.

Once we love ourselves, only then can others love us. People can only give to us that which we give to ourselves.

Time now for each of us to think of ourselves as much as we do others and enjoy a calmer, more honourable ride with our wishes at the forefront. If we are happy, everyone around us will be happy.

Daily affirmations, week 42

1

When things go wrong, you see very definitely what you do not want, therefore clarifying what you do want.

2

There are no mistakes when something doesn't work out. Know a better way is being found.

3

Life is always moving in the direction of your dreams, even if it sometimes takes you in the opposite direction for a while.

4

The moment you put out a request to the universe, it's on its way.

5

The only thing that delays your requests are your thoughts telling you how impossible they are to achieve.

Your Weekly Wonder 42

The universe is always bringing your deepest wishes to you.

If you have been waiting a long time for something, do not resent the time taken. Know that whatever you have asked for is on its way, but the end result has to be the best outcome for everyone concerned and there is often a lot of juggling to be done.

Sometimes we have to make a lot of changes in ourselves to morph into what we are asking for because we have to be on the same vibrational frequency of what we are wanting to attract in.

For example we cannot ask for financial security and continually worry about what bills we have to pay: this cancels out our request for abundance and immediately puts forward a request for more bills to pay, more lack, the opposite of what we want.

We have to fine-tune to attract what we are wanting and be ever vigilant with our thoughts. Remember, you never get what you want, you get what you are; therefore you have to become what you are wanting.

Going back to our example of thinking more abundantly, a good way to change our thinking and become what we are wanting would be to be grateful for services that we have received, perhaps gas or electricity, before we offered any payment, realising that the person who has given us the service trusts that we have the financial wherewithal to pay what we owe, and therefore they see us as abundant; and so we are now on the frequency of having, which is where we want to be.

A request from the universe is never denied, but often delayed until we catch up with it or while the fine tuning takes place in our thinking so we are on the same vibrational frequency to magnetize the new conditions to us.

If we ask for an ideal mate but then feel lonely, we will only have more loneliness. We get what we are thinking, so we must find things that are fun to do alone or with friends, and our ideal mate has to step in because our every request is heard.

When we are enjoying ourselves we are on the same frequency of having what we want, and it has to step in. Just pretend until it happens.

The universe doesn't know the difference between fantasy and reality, negative and positive; it will just send what you are thinking the most. That is where the time issue comes in: if we could spend more time thinking of how good we'll feel when we have what we want, it could come *immediately because we would have no opposing thoughts to cancel it out.*

The fastest way to fine-tune is to find some-thing in the moment to enjoy while you are waiting, to enjoy and appreciate the conditions that you find yourself in now, looking forward to the new that you are asking for and knowing that when the time is right and you are ready it will arrive. If you were ready it would be here.

When you are enjoying yourself now, more is sent for you to enjoy, and since what you are requesting is top of the list, it has to come.

The secret is to feel good no matter what.

Always reach for something that makes you feel good, because that is how you will feel when you have what you want, then you will only attract more in that feels good.

The universe has your request, it will come, it is the law. Like attracts like.

Daily affirmations, week 43

1

Always go with what is in front of you.

2

*You don't need to search for your good,
it's always there close by.
Follow what gives a skip to your heart.*

3

Try to say "yes" more to life.

4

*Have no fixed idea how your "good" ought to
come. It will come in the most magical way if you
let go any attachment to "how" it has to come.*

5

*Know that whatever you wish for is on its way.
Appreciation and expectation speed up the process
big time.*

Your Weekly Wonder 43

If something is meant for you, you cannot lose it. If it isn't meant for you, you won't want it.

There are no mistakes in life. Nothing ever goes wrong. Everything that happens is moving us towards what we most want in the fastest way and we never get it done. There is always more to have, be or experience.

Any change that comes in your life is always good.

Anything that leaves your life is always replaced by something better, even if you are the one who pushes it away.

Know life is always moving forward, always getting better.

You cannot lose anything that is meant for you. If it is not meant for you, you won't want it.

Life is always a win-win situation. Know whatever is happening is meant to be happening to lead you where you most want to be. Trust the process. You can't get it wrong.

To make life more comfortable and bring what you want quicker, see good in every situation. Look for the benefit, no matter how deeply hidden. It is always there. Look for the good everywhere, see it in everything and that is what will come to you. The only reason it is ever missing is because the thoughts we have about the impossibility of *what we want get in the way.*

Forget logic, work with magic. Just concentrate on what you want. The universe will work out 'how'.

That's not your job.

If you can imagine something you can have it.

Keep imagining.

Daily affirmations, week 44

1

Be ready to receive your good.

2

Keep your wishes secret until they appear.
Then you can tell the whole world.

3

Watch out for any leads to follow. They will
appear as "hunches", good things to do.

4

Look for demonstrations that your dreams are
coming about: synchronistic events or unlikely
communications connected to your dream.

5

Think of all the good things that have come about
already in your life. Like attracts like: this will
bring more good things to you.

Your Weekly Wonder 44

Your natural state is joy. When we are joyous our bodies thrive.

Each tiny cell exudes a honey-like liquid that keep us healthy and glowing, thriving and buoyant.

When we are nervous, anxious, frightened, stressed, each cell exudes a caustic liquid that attacks and destroys our vibrant selves and we become ill.

We cannot afford the luxury of a negative thought.

Look around you at peoples' expressions, their faces: those who are happy and choose joyful thoughts have smooth line-free faces full of glowing love of life.

They thrive and you can see that in the way they move and talk no matter what age they are.

There is always a choice. Even if we cannot at the moment change our course of life, we can in this moment choose our attitude to it, which paradoxically will change our reality.

As thoughts are things, if we choose happy ones we will attract a reality that supports our new feelings.

Daily affirmations, week 45

1

Be happy for no reason.

2

Expect things to work out.

3

Follow your good.

4

There's always time for everything.

5

Make a decision to look for the good in everything.

Your Weekly Wonder 45

Life continues to be overwhelming for most of us, even though we have this promise of a new vibrational frequency stepping in and bringing a smoother ride.

This is a good thing. It brings to the surface from the depth of our being any hidden fears, traumas, resentments that are unreleased. We have no need to analyse them, only to release them. The clearest, most effective way to release them is through movement, running, yoga, dancing, martial arts, rugby, football, cricket, anything you love that gets you moving.

This feeling of being overwhelmed, although very uncomfortable, releases a powerful desire in us for what would bring us peace, and this turbo-charges us onto the new frequency of allowing it.

I feel we are all fine-tuning to enable us to jump on board this new frequency so we can be carried along on a warm slipstream to the new futures we have all been creating. Like spring bursting round us it is here and we cannot escape our good so long as we don't lose faith on the way with the long wait !

Try to drop all the frantic racing round with all the meaningless tasks. They just waste time and energy with worry and anxiety on how to complete or make things happen.

This is the old way and no longer appropriate.

We are stepping into a new easier, more joyful way to live, doing very little but accomplishing a lot more. If we don't start doing this, following our joy, our bliss, just like getting used to computer technology we'll be left behind.

Just do what you feel like doing each day, one task at a time, all that needs to be done will be done and the rest is not your job. Hand it over at the end of the day to the universe. Either someone else will do it or you will be inspired to do it in a good relaxed way and it will be done in half the time.

Stress, anxiety, worry is a thing of the past, achieves nothing, just makes us older and tired. Let it go. Choose calm, joy, fun, excitement, bliss, abundance, giving, loving, openness, a life full and overflowing with all good things.

Daily affirmations, week 46

1

*If you keep doing the same things,
you'll get the same results.*

2

*Make small changes today. Wear something you
don't normally wear. Walk instead of drive. Have
something different for lunch.*

3

*Take baby steps towards planning something big
you've been wanting for a while.
For example, stop by the travel agent and pick up
that brochure on Bali.*

4

*Write a list of ten things you would like to change
in your life. Sit back and watch it happen.*

5

*Enjoy what you already have in front of you.
This is your fast forward button.*

Your Weekly Wonder 46

*In life everything is on offer to you all the time:
possessions, people, qualities. Be ready to receive
anything from anywhere at any time. Have no
fixed ideas of how it should come or from where;
this blocks the flow and stops the magic. All you
have to do is be ready to take action, to allow it,
when it appears.*

*Your job is only knowing that what you have
asked for is out there, believing you can have it
and allowing it when it comes.*

Daily affirmations, week 47

1

*If you want others to change, change yourself.
They will respond differently.*

2

*If you keep doing the same things, you'll get the
same results.*

3

If you want change, reinvent yourself.

4

*By knowing what you don't want,
you know what you do. The opposite !*

5

Change can be easy. Just imagine the end result.

Your Weekly Wonder 47

What would you like from life?

   Can you remember?

   Are you so busy doing stuff for others that you have forgotten yourself?

   Who are you?

   Do you smile at yourself as you see your reflection in the mirror?

   Tell yourself how well you have done?

   How far you have come? How proud you are of yourself? Just for turning up every day?

   Do you think of yourself at all in good ways or do you just remind yourself how little you have accomplished, how hard life is, that no one understands you, others have more than you, are luckier etc.

   Step over to the other side and remind yourself there is no such thing as luck.

People get the results from life that they expect. If you decide to be 'lucky' right now, that is what you will start to experience.

   Decide you are always lucky, that everything comes easily to you, it always has. Start telling a better-feeling story about yourself, your life, your world. The universe doesn't know the difference between fantasy and reality; it will just send what you are thinking.

Start to think of what you want rather than the opposite and watch your reality change magically into one full of all the good stuff you have been watching others enjoy.

There is no limit – if you can imagine it, you can have it. Just allow it, don't block it with thoughts of it not being possible.

As Goethe said, if you have a dream, a wish, a desire for anything, you always have the wherewithal to achieve it.

Go for it.

Daily affirmations, week 48

1

Your thoughts are everything. Choose them wisely.

2

What you are thinking right now is what you are setting up. Is it what you want?

3

Monitor your thoughts.

4.

The universe doesn't recognise any difference between fantasy or reality. It will send what you are thinking.

5

The universe doesn't recognise any difference between positive or negative. It will send what you are thinking.

Your Weekly Wonder 48

*If you feel people are treating you badly, taking
you for granted, behaving in a disrespectful way,
where have you given them permission to do so?*

*What vibes are you sending out about who you
are and how to treat you and why are you
attracting these people into your life?*

*If this is happening to you and if you are still
reading, it probably is . . . Take a step back and
look at the way you treat yourself.*

Are you taking care of you?

Are you respecting yourself?

Are you giving yourself a hard time?

Are you giving yourself time and attention?

*First of all you must honour and respect
yourself before others can do so. You show people
how to treat you by the way you treat yourself.*

*When you honour and respect yourself, your
needs, your life, others will honour and make time
for you in the same way.*

*Most of us put others first and then wonder
why we start to feel resentful and left out. People
around us are only following our lead and
treating us the way we treat ourselves.*

There is no reward and punishment system.

Put your own needs first, you will then come from a powerful place of having all your needs met and people will follow your lead and treat you well.

You can then give happily to others.

Daily affirmations, week 49

1

If something isn't working out for you, aim higher. You're not asking for enough.

2

Always see the bigger picture. Sometimes when things "go wrong" it's a short cut.

3

Have faith that life is good.

4

Look for the good. It's always there.

5

Everyone is always doing the best they can with the knowledge they have.

Your Weekly Wonder 49

It's all about the journey and enjoying the process.

You are never going to get there. When you get 'there' it will be another here and again you'll be looking over there.

Enjoy every day, don't wait until you get 'there' to enjoy yourself. Don't put life on hold until you've left school, got the qualifications, moved house, got the ideal partner, fitness, discovered your life purpose.

Whatever it is you are struggling towards stop the struggle, you can't get to joy through struggle. It doesn't work like that. You can only get to joy through joy, through accessing a place that feels good to you.

It is a choice you make to feel good no matter what. That is what brings joy to you.

It doesn't mean bad things won't happen or that you become some 'la la land' idiot with his head in the sand.

It means that you trust the universe to bring you your good and that all things happen for a reason. Even the so-called 'bad' things all happen for a reason.

If you look for the good it is always there, in every situation, we can't always see where the gift is until later, but it is always there.

Move quickly back to joy no matter what is

happening in the fastest way you can, then more joy will come to you.

You get what you think about. Therefore you cannot afford the luxury of being miserable, especially when what you are miserable about is probably a good thing anyway – and even maybe a short cut to what you want.

Daily affirmations, week 50

1

Try to have patience with others. The more difficult a person is being, the more they are asking for love.

2

Ask "how can I open my heart here and be more loving?" Go the extra mile.

3

Always give that little bit more, for a birthday gift or a tip to a taxi driver. Give that little bit extra.

4

Walk away rather than criticize or snap back.

5

Be the change you want.

Your Weekly Wonder 50

The most important thing in life is that you are happy, joyful. More joy can only come from joy. You cannot get to joy through struggle. It doesn't work like that.

You can only get to joy through joy, doing something you love.

To be healthy you have to be happy. It is the only way. Joy is the answer to everything. Doing what you love to do, following your bliss.

If you are happy everyone around you will be happy. You somehow allow them to be happy also.

We have all been taught to put others first and have lost the childlike way we had of always doing what we wanted to do.

We no longer trust ourselves to know what we want. We have been taught even to do the opposite. We are told we are too much, too loud, too messy, too demanding, but only because it didn't suit others for us to be the way that felt best for us, it didn't fit in with what they wanted. We started to behave in a certain way to fit in because we wanted to be loved and our survival depended on it. No one meant to mislead us, they were just teaching us how they had been taught to fit in, to be accepted, and they thought they were helping us. They were keen to tell us the rules, looking right and left before crossing the road etc., but when it came to allowing us to be who we wanted to be it all got a little sticky.

We are no longer those children and have no need to be the product of that childhood. We are grown up now and can choose how to be, what to do, how to act in ways that please us.

Throw off this cloak camouflaging your true self. Smile again with blissful joy of being you. Go find your bliss.

Daily affirmations, week 51

1

Try to relate only a good story of your life.

2

Try to talk about happy, successful things.

3

Try to emphasize the good.

4

*If you can't think of anything nice to say,
don't say anything at all.*

5

Whatever you give out always comes back to you.

Your Weekly Wonder 51

Try to understand everyone is doing the best they can with the knowledge they have. We all are.

You cannot put someone right by telling them how to behave. It doesn't work.

If we want change, we have to be the change we want.

Try not to judge or criticise another's behaviour, otherwise you are attracting in criticism for yourself.

Try not to have to fight your corner, otherwise you'll always be in a position of having to defend yourself.

Love yourself enough to walk away and not put yourself in the position of bad guy.

Any accusing or negative energy you hurl at others has to come back to you, no matter how justified you think it is. The price you have to pay is too high.

Whatever you do or say to others comes back like a boomerang, only far stronger.

This goes for good or bad intentions you throw out. Stay with the good ones and receive only those back, multiplied. It's a much better idea, no matter how tempting it is at the time to react !

Try to be more understanding of others for your health's sake. You are the one whose blood pressure will be raised.

Anger is not conducive to good health. Express it in a healthy way: running, squash, kick-boxing, punching the bed, anything that is safe and not hurled at another person either with words or actions; not because you are a "goody two-shoes" but because you know how the universe works & you know your thoughts or actions will come back to you big time. Therefore you love yourself enough to walk away from anything destructive & give it no thought.

Know that a person who is being difficult is always a fearful person and struggling somewhere.

The more difficult a person is the more they need love and understanding.

You don't have to be the one to give them that but love yourself enough to walk away so you are not affected by them in any way that can hurt you.

The most important thing is that you feel good. It is possible all the time, we just have to think in different ways.

Be the bigger person. Show the way. It's not easy, but it's the only way if we want to be happy.

Daily affirmations, week 52

1

*The only thing that stops your good coming to you
are your thoughts against it.*

2

*Look for the good in every situation.
It's always there.*

3

*Life rarely works out the way you expect:
it's always better.*

4

Everything is a mirror for you.

5

*Whenever you see something you like in others,
you see yourself.*

Your Weekly Wonder 52: Christmas message

Babies are often referred to as "bundles of joy."
Well, you're also a delightful present to others – you too are joy, gift wrapped in a beautiful human body.

Everywhere you go, you exude wonderful energies, even when you're unaware of this process. You can't help but spread happiness as that's your true essence and nature.

Of course you can increase or decrease the amount of joy that you radiate, so place your attention on showering huge amounts of bliss wherever you go. You can do this without a word – without even being noticed. Simply set your attention throughout the day to spread happy feelings and it is done. You'll know by the smiles and laughter you inspire that your aim has been fulfilled, for these are reflections of the gift you have given.

Thoughts are everything.
Make sure yours are good !!

Printed in Great Britain
by Amazon

68623970R00083